Small Town Girl

Poems on solitude, strength, and stardust.

Priyanka Naik

BookLeaf Publishing

India | USA | UK

Made with ❤ on the BookLeaf Publishing Platform
www.bookleafpub.in
www.bookleafpub.com

Dedication

To poetry,
for helping me confront, challenge,
and cherish life.

Preface

I have always believed that small towns shape people in ways the world doesn't always recognize. They teach you patience in their quiet streets, resilience in their stillness, and a kind of wonder that comes from watching the same sky day after day, yet never quite seeing it the same way. They do not rush you forward, but they plant something restless in your soul, a longing not just to leave, but to understand, to reach beyond what is familiar without forgetting where you began.

This book is a collection of those moments—of solitude that strengthens, of dreams that refuse to fade, of an ordinary girl who carries the sky inside her.

The poems in these pages are for those who have ever felt too small for the world yet too vast for its confines. For those who know that strength doesn't always roar; it also exists in quiet defiance, in soft persistence, in the refusal to break.

I hope my poems find you when you need them most. And I hope, in their lines, you see a reflection of your own journey; the solitude you've embraced, the strength you've built, and the stardust you've never stopped carrying.

--- *Priyanka*

Acknowledgements

First and foremost, I thank the omnipotent, omniscient, omnipresent God I believe in - without His grace, this book could not have been written.

To my parents, for giving me both roots and wings, for instilling in me the confidence to touch the skies but also the humility to stay grounded. Your love, your sacrifices, and your unwavering belief in me have shaped the person I am and the words I write.

To my sibling, the one who has seen me in both light and shadow, who understands my silences as much as my words. Thank you for the conversations; the arguments that sharpen wit and thought, and the rare but necessary reminders not to take myself too seriously.

And finally, to you, the reader. Whether you stumbled upon this book by chance or sought it out with purpose, thank you. Words find meaning in the spaces they fill, and by reading my verses, you make my poems whole.
This book is as much yours as it is mine.

First aid to a breaking heart

Every minute, a new heart breaks
And someone tries to move on
Stop wasting your time on
barren soil that refuses to harvest
anything but your tears.
Concentrate instead on how
you can transform
into the fertile pastures of promise
you made to yourself.
Sow the seeds of your dreams
and water them, watch them sprout
Into lush foliage, tend to it alone if you must.
Until you find someone you can trust
to water your soul, strengthen your roots,
polish your hesitant shine,
who will love you,
for the rainforest you have become.
Hearts break, people heal,
and along the way you meet a friend.
Along the way you find yourself!

Casual Observations

An idea stirs, restless in the morning light.
A half-written poem given up mid-thought.
The day exhales.

A slice of bread drops to the floor;
The smallest betrayals go unnoticed.

Outside, the wind turns.
A kite dips, then rises higher; unfettered.
Some things stumble.
Some things learn to soar.

To Kill a Mocking Word

You call me names, you roll your eyes,
You sneer, you spit, you weave your lies.
You want a war? You crave the fight?
You burn with rage, I shine with light
You throw your words like jagged stones,
Sharp as knives, cold as bones.
But I don't bleed, I don't break,
Your hate's a ripple, my calm's a lake

You mock, you hiss, you bare your teeth,
Waiting for my wrath beneath.
I meet your storm with steady grace,
Not a grimace on my face
Your words may burn, but I won't fold,
I stand in light, serene and bold.
A peaceful smile, a glance so still,
Soft as silk, but iron-willed
I do not bow, I do not kneel,
I let you rage, I let you heal.

For all your thunder, all your storm,
Your cruelest words will lose their form.

For a mocking word, once meant to win,
Finds no fuel and dies within.

Small Town Girl

I am the pearl the ocean never boasts of,
hidden in an oyster no one stops to open.
No flash, no fire;
just the slow patience of waves shaping me,
grain by grain, into something exquisite.
I do not glimmer in the city's neon glow.
My light is quieter;
like the silver of moonlit fields,
like the gold of wheat bending in the wind.

I wear the sky's colors,
earthy and unafraid,
feet rooted in roads that remember my steps.
I speak like rivers cutting through stone,
soft, relentless, honest.
I will look into your eyes and not look away,
for I have never learned
to drape my truth in velvet,
never learned to bow to empty glitter.

Yes, I dream of constellations,
but I do not beg the stars to fall.
I build my ladders with my own hands,

climbing, slipping, climbing again,
never once taking flight on borrowed wings.

6

They see a quiet girl, plain as rain,
but let them sit in my storm.
Let them hear the thunder in my words,
feel the currents in my mind,
and they will know;
still waters do not mean safe.

Yes, I hold too tightly.
Yes, I love like wildfire.
Yes, I burn,
but tell me, what is a pearl,
if not the ghost of a wound that refused to fester?

Holi Unplugged

Not from packets, not from powders,
today, let us play with the colors of the earth.
Bring me the saffron fire of the marigold tree,
ablaze in the afternoon sun,
its petals falling like tiny flames onto the wind.
Dip your hands into the crimson flush of Gulmohars,
their branches whispering stories of summer.
Let the Parijatak bless the dawn with its ivory touch,
stars fallen softly upon dewy grass,
their fragrance a hymn to the morning air.
Smear the sky's cerulean hush across your palms,
watch it ripple in the waters,
a liquid mirror of endless blue.
Pluck the tender green of mango leaves,
crushed between fingers, their scent alive;
a promise of spring folded in their veins.
Let peacock feathers brush our cheeks
with the iridescence of monsoon secrets,
shimmering between blue and green,
as if the sky has hidden its laughter in their shine.
The golden wheat sways like a thousand lamps,
fields aflame in the song of the sun.
The earth wears *sindoor* where the palash trees bloom,

a crimson tide against the brown of her skin.
And when the night arrives,
let us paint each other in moonlight,
silver strokes of quiet love,
while the fireflies dance,
scattering stars upon our shoulders.
For why wait for a single day
when the earth plays Holi in every season?
The amber of autumn leaves,
the winter snow like powdered pearls,
the springtime blush of wild hibiscus,
the monsoon's emerald breath upon the hills,
everywhere, always, colors bloom.
Dip your hands in the rivers of dawn,
stain your feet in the rust of falling leaves,
let the sky, the trees, the wind;
let life itself color you.
Not from packets, not from powders,
but from the hands of the earth,
let us play Holi, not just today, but every day,
all year round.

Reminder

In all relations, that we choose,
this much we ought to know;
In which we need to win or lose,
and which in time let go.

What Slipped Away

I scribble a list on the back of an old receipt;
milk, bread, peppermint chocolate,
the essentials and the indulgences,
a map to follow through the labyrinth of choice.
But the supermarket stretches, endless, bright,
aisles folding into one another,
each shelf a promise, each row a temptation.
Peppermint waits, steady, sure,
but beside it—dark caramel, milk and sea salt,
chili-kissed, almond-crushed, praline-smooth,
each whispering, each promising
a taste of something different.
I reach, I pause, I waver, I forget.
Indecision lingers, thick as air.
Milk—skimmed, full-fat, almond, oat.
Cartons that question.
Bread---sourdough, whole wheat, pumpernickel.
Grains I cannot even name.
Something new.
Something else.
Not what I came for.
And yet, I find

at checkout, a stranger's choice in my cart,
the taste of something I never wanted.

Small Big Joys - the 'Goan' way

In my hometown,
people find joy in the smallest things.
A stroll along the Mandovi
is no less than walking by the Seine,
except here, the river hums in Konkani,
and the scent of salt and cashew feni
hangs in the air like a forgotten song.

Here, life is unhurried, a melody in no rush,
where mornings begin with chit-chat over fresh poi,
and evenings drift into laughter over cutlet pao,
or a quiet stroll by the beach,
ending with the comfort of a ros-omelette dinner,
spiced with stories and the hush of the waves.

To be Goan is to pause;
to marvel at the strokes of Mario Miranda,
where every caricature tells a truth,
to lose yourself in the hues of Laxman Pai,
to feel the spirit of Angelo da Fonseca
etched in every chapel's quiet embrace.

We love deeply and argue freely,
our voices rising like the tide,
only to recede just as fast,
leaving no trace of discord,
only the warmth of understanding.
Here, grudges, like footprints in the sand;
are washed away before the day is done.

My Goa is a rhythm, a way of being,
a longing for fish curry when away too long,
a sigh at the sight of coconut trees
leaning lazily over red-tiled homes,
the sight of old balcao, where neighbours sit,
rocking gently, trading stories with the wind,
as if time itself, like them, is in no hurry to move.

We have carved our own place in the world,
not with noise, but with music,
not with haste, but with the quiet certainty
of church bells echoing through sleepy villages,
a sound that lingers long after it fades.

The world may spin, but my Goa sways;
slow, steady, sun-drenched,
wrapped in the warmth of a *susegaad* afternoon,
where happiness is not something we seek,
but something we have always known.

For here in my hometown,
people find joy in the smallest things.

Untitled

Sunlight streams in through the window blinds,
casting silver lines across the room.

There are cookie boxes on the floor,
toppled and forgotten,
and a couple of apricot cans lie unopened,
past their expiry date.

The fog has lifted,
and the past whispers to the present,
"Now is your only guarantee—don't wait."

Unapologetic

I will not apologise
For the honesty of my thoughts;
the ones that made you confront
your punctured soul,
that shattered the fragile walls of your ego.

I will not apologise
for holding up the mirror
to the beast you had become.

I will not apologise
for guarding my conscience
while you bartered yours
for cherry trees,
for refusing to be encased
in your fabricated world of words
with my voice ringing true, untamed.

I will not apologise
for leaving you behind;
your palm had outgrown mine,
and I longed to float
while you grew roots

in all the wrong places.

So when you see me now,
that wistful look upon your face,
a silent echo of what could have been,
I smile, but I will not apologise.
For we made our choices
and I will not apologise
for choosing me before you.

(This poem is an ode to all those relationships that end with relief and not regret. Some lessons are learned the hard way. Loving yourself is one of them.)

Somewhere, Almost Heaven

There is a place I long to find,
a dream that lingers in my mind.
Where silkworms weave their golden thread,
soft as words once left unsaid.
Where the air is silk, and rivers sing,
a hush as light as a butterfly's wing.
where flowers spill their scent so sweet,
where earth and sky and longing meet.
Where jasmine whispers, roses sigh,
and violets drift as winds pass by.
Their perfume wraps the world in lace,
a fleeting touch, a lost embrace.
And countless fireflies in endless flight,
scatter kisses made of light.
Where the wind hums low, the waters call,
a song half-known, yet loved by all.
I taste the moon, its silver glow,
a warmth my heart has come to know.

Yet is it real? Or just a trace
of something time cannot replace?
Still, I wander, still, I roam,
chasing echoes far from home.

A place unseen, yet feels so deep,
a whispered dream I long to keep.

19

On Free Will

What is this weight in your hands,
this trembling thing you call choice?
Do you not see how the trees, even as they stand,
lean toward the light; not by command,
but by longing?

And you;
you say you are bound,
that the road was written
before your feet ever touched it.
But who, then, is the writer?
Who is the hand that moves across the page
If not your own?
A single breath, a glance held too long,
a word spoken or left unsaid;
and suddenly, the sky shifts,
the ground beneath you is no longer the same.
What was certain becomes uncertain,
what was near slips away,
what was distant now reaches for you.

Fate is not just the river that carries you,
but also the moment you choose

to step into its current.
The wind does not ask where it must go;
it listens, it turns, it learns the shape
of the world, it hangs on to a stronger faith.
And so must you,
if you are to be more than silence.
Look;
even the stars, though ancient,
still burn anew each night.

Reminiscence

Childhood memories,
Immune to time and termite,
Like the dear dolls we'd hide
behind as children.
Imperishable, indestructible
Some spelled to furnish our homes,
Some to warm our hearts.
Echoes of laughter,
whispers of secrets,
Tales spun in the fabric of twilight.
Each thread, a story stitched
into the quilt of our past.
The scent of old books,
the touch of weathered wood,
All holding the essence
of days gone by.
We carry them, not as burdens,
but as treasures,
In the pockets of our minds,
Where time cannot reach,
And love remains,
Undimmed by the passing years.

No Ordinary Love

Some love is a steady flame,
burning low but never fading,
a warm hand to hold through the years,
a rhythm that hums like an old song,
familiar, unshaken.
But we;
we are a flickering lantern in the wind,
bright, then dim, then burning wild,
dancing between shadow and fire,
never quite still.

Some love is a river,
flowing smooth, certain of its course,
carving out forever in gentle persistence.
But we;
we are the ocean in a storm,
rising, crashing,
then pulling back into calm,
our tempests as much a part of us
as our still waters.

Some love is a story written in even lines,
each chapter leading to the next,

a tale that time will tell without hesitation.
But we;
we are scribbled notes in the margins,
half-finished sentences, crossed-out words,
a story that changes every time it's read.

And maybe that is why we hold on,
why we keep coming back,
why this love, chaotic as it is, still makes sense,
It is the inconsistencies that define us.

Recurring

25

Some goodbyes are never said,
some need not be said,
some cannot be said,
and some despite
being bid a million times,
are fated to happen again.

The Great Sunday Hoax

Morning unfolds in quiet hush,
light draping the walls in a slow embrace,
a promise of rest, a whisper of ease.
But the kettle hisses, the sink sighs,
the floor begs for sweeping,
the laundry waits, patient yet insistent.

I think—maybe later,
I will sit by the window,
watch the world move without me.

One task spills into another;
a cup left on the table,
a stain on the counter,
a tangle of wires to unknot,
a cupboard door slightly ajar.
Each one small, each one nothing,
each one stealing a minute, a breath.

Not now, but soon,
I will stretch, breathe,
let silence settle into my bones.

Midday arrives unnoticed,
the sun high but irrelevant,
because the bed sheets still need changing,
the plants are thirsty,
the fridge hums its disapproval
at the empty milk carton.

I remind myself---later,
I will read, just a few pages,
just a moment to slip away.

Just one more thing;
a cloth to wipe, a chair to straighten,
a call to return, a shelf to fix.
Just one more, and then,
then I will sit.

But evening creeps in while I fold,
fresh laundry stacked in quiet surrender,
iron-warmed shirts smoothed and tucked away.
A quick meal, something simple;
because hunger does not wait,
because even an empty stomach
demands to be fed.

Soon, I tell myself,
I will close my eyes,

let sleep find me before the week does.

Then stocking the fridge for the week ahead,
lining up bottles, stacking vegetables,
checking dates, tossing what's old.
A light bulb flickers, replace it.
The garbage bin fills, take it out.
A sock is missing, find it.

And somewhere before I even notice,
Sunday slips, like an oasis on the horizon,
shimmering in the distance,
fading the moment I draw near,
a dream of water in a desert of days,
never real enough to touch.

Dichotomy of Light

Do not undermine the power of light.
It can expose and deceive.
It can create illusions and shadows.
It can enter a tear drop
and emerge as a rainbow.
Light can be illuminating
It can sometimes be blinding too.
It can lift up your deadened spirit
but can also make your eyes sting.
It can amplify your best features.
It can highlight your worst scars.
It can brighten up your carefully shot pictures
But may also overexpose the lens and distort the image.

Light is a similie .
Light is a metaphor.
But light is a paradox too.
It is everything and nothing at once;
ask someone who is blind from birth.
Ask the creatures of the night,
the firefly, the Parijat tree,
the child who is afraid of the dark,
the woman who takes the last local,

the rooster who wakes the world at dawn.
And then ask light itself whether it is content
at its fickle ways, at the duplicity it represents.

For light needs darkness as companion
Not to undermine its power
but to remind it of its weakness,
to reflect its strength.
It is often lonely and has no desire
to shimmer alone in its triumph.

And Yet

Your name hums in the rush of the city,
slips through the cracks of a stranger's voice,
flickers in headlights, in half-lit signs.

I see you in faces that are not yours,
reach for shadows that do not stay.
I lose you a hundred times a day.

To the Daughters of the World

To the daughters of this waking world,
let no chain call itself love,
let no silence be mistaken for peace.
Unfurl your voice like a blade.
Wear your defiance like armor.
Beauty is a trick they taught you to chase.
Courage is the pulse beneath your skin.

You are not here to be admired,
to be measured,
to be kept.
You are here to burn,
to carve your name into the marrow of time,
to taste the air unshackled.

Do not soften your tongue to soothe them.
Do not shrink your body to fit their hands.
If they call you too much,
too wild,
too unyielding,
take it as a crown.

Run, not like the hunted,
but like the storm.
Run, not to escape,
but to claim what is yours.
Run until the earth remembers your name,
until the wind carries your war-cry,
until the meek thing inside you
becomes the goddess you were always meant to be.

Flower Power

There is a story behind every flower;
Of how it started out as just a seed
that got buried deep, under pressure
or maybe carelessly strewn around
in the grand expanses of the wild,
or the confined spaces of a clay pot
in your balcony, receiving the warmth
of the sun shining overhead,
watered by nature or a garden hose.
The seed grows into a plant.
The plant grows into a tree.
Its roots spreading, holding soil.
Its branches gathering a bit of sky.
Come spring and it will flower,
paying obeisance to the sun.
The plant in your balcony,
the tree in your backyard,
tended, untended, both will shower
love and hope to one and all.

There is a story behind every flower;
one that is rooted in the ground,
with its fragrance spread all around.

It will bloom, and speak out the truth,
for all the seasons it has felt,
for all the trials it has faced.
There is a story behind every flower;
Of chance, of birth by serendipity.
Of choice, of survival, of strength.
To continue even after it has wilted.
To inspire even after it is dead.

There is a story behind every flower;
Of fury, of anger, of dismay
at those who had ignored its struggle,
and just when it had started to bloom,
nipped it in the bud; a life interrupted.
There is a story behind every flower;
the one in your balcony, or in the wild,
or even the one you have pressed in this book,
if only we have the time to listen,
if only we have the will to learn.

A Study In Longing

When I think of us, I see
a Matisse afternoon,
all bright colors and reckless laughter,
our voices moving like cutouts of light,
shifting, reshaping the sky.

Our hands wandering
like Klimt's brushstrokes,
tracing gilded secrets along each other's skin,
each touching a whisper of something sacred,
something the world was never meant to see.

When we laughed,
we were a Chagall sky,
floating weightless in some impossible blue,
our joy an oxbow moon,
bending time around us.

When we held each other,
I swear I heard Egon Schiele's lines tremble,
raw and aching,
the urgency of two figures
daring to belong to the same world.

And when we parted,
we became Picasso's shifting light,
fragmented but never lost,
our edges rearranging, searching for form,
as if love had to break and reassemble
just to prove it was real.

We were Vermeer's quiet radiance,
bathed in the glow of moments too soft to name.
We were Van Gogh's fevered sky,
swirling with the madness of love too vast to hold.
We were Dali's liquid time,
melting between dreams and the warmth of our touch.
We were Munch's silent cry,
aching with the weight of what was left unsaid.
We were Frida's tangled roots,
growing into and through each other's pain.
We were Degas' fleeting embrace,
a moment of beauty always on the verge of vanishing.

When I think of us,
I see a canvas left unfinished,
colors still wet, still running,
as if even art could not contain us,
as if love, in its truest form,
was always meant to blur into memory.

After-taste

It used to be my favorite snack;
red, clumpy, speckled with fruit,
a sweet delight spread thick and smooth
on soft white bread, cut into neat triangles,
stacked with care in a Mickey Mouse tiffin,
pink and white, snug in my schoolbag.

At recess, I'd pry open the lid,
inhale the sugar-scented promise,
the sticky joy of childhood afternoons
sealed between slices, waiting for me.

But today, I traveled back in time,
unlatching the past with eager hands,
and stole a bite from memory's plate,
the tiffin, half-eaten, waiting still.

The bread had stiffened, the jam turned dark,
its once-sweet tang now bitter on my tongue.
And in that single, lingering taste,
I understood what childhood never warned;
that some flavors fade, some joys sour,

and growing up is nothing more
than learning how to stomach the change.

Disillusioned

As a child, I believed
in a tooth fairy
who'd quietly visit in the night
And while I was sleeping,
replace my fallen tooth,
with a gift pressed under my pillow
As an adult, I learned
all losses are not so reversible.

I

Glistening fresh on rose petals red,
I am the words you left unsaid.
I am the morning drop of dew.
I am the sun that shines anew.
I am the tree that screens the light .
I am the dawn at the end of night.
I am the bird that skims the clouds
I am the tiger amidst the shrouds.
I am the rain drop on your pane.
I am the snow that blocks your lane.
I am winter, summer, autumn, spring.
I am the melody in the songs you sing.
I am the wilting rose, the blooming bud.
I am the lotus in the mud.
I am the poet and the lines he writes.
I am the soldier and the war he fights.
I am the good and the evil too.
I am me but I'm also you.
So when you strike with a blow unkind,
Or a hurtful barb, bear this in mind;
It's not just me that you curse,
You attack the entire universe.

Anatomy of Rebellion

42

Wake up, it's your life, not theirs.
Don't bow, don't kneel, don't yield to the shadows.
Grab the reins, spit into the jaws of the beast.
You and you alone are the captain of this tide.

Life will throw punches, its tempests will rage wild
but you, you stand unshaken, grounded.
And laugh, laugh in the face of this storm,
for the only surrender is in silence.

They will name you reckless, call you ruin-bound.
But what do they know of hunger, of fire in the blood?
Of those who walk unshod through embers,
and leave footprints of light in their wake?

Don't hand over your armor.
Don't let them carve your soul.
Be fierce, be crazy, be unapologetic.
This is your story, own it, damn it,
you only have one shot.